SECOND INNINGS ON YOUR TERMS!

Dedicated to

To all the readers of my previous book,

Retire on Your Terms: A Guide to Holistic Retirement

*Your positive reviews and support encouraged
me to continue this journey*

Thank you for being a part of this story

Retire on Your Terms is available globally
on Amazon. Please scan this QR code if
you want to Purchase on Amazon India.

SECOND INNINGS ON YOUR TERMS!

PASSIONATE RETIREMENT FOR LIFE

RAJESH MINOCHA

ISBN: 978-81-987425-7-5

Published by
VerseWave: Crafting Your Story
Belghoria, Kolkata, WB 700056
Website: www.versewavepublishing.com

Testimonial

In his book, **Second Innings on Your Terms**, Rajesh Minocha writes in a style that is both evocative and structured. The tone is optimistic and the content informative. He addresses the issues that face retirees and outlines sharp and succinct solutions to help navigate this phase of transition. The book serves as a ready reckoner for those planning to step out of their primary careers, on the brink of a major change or already retired, and presents a well-crafted summary of ideas to navigate the path ahead.

The ten chapters in the book deal with the aspects of retirement, from rediscovering purpose to building strong relationships and everything else in between. The reader will view retirement from a new perspective – as an exciting new journey with myriad opportunities for personal growth and meaningful pursuits.

WisdomCircle wishes Rajesh Minocha much success in his endeavour.

Swati Diwakar
Lead – Learning and Development
WisdomCircle

"More than a book on money. It's a guide to living your second innings with meaning."

Second Innings on Your Terms is a thoughtful companion for anyone moving from professional deadlines to a life of meaningful choices. Rajesh Minocha goes beyond finances, addressing the emotional, psychological, and lifestyle shifts that retirement brings, which are often overlooked but deeply felt.

Whether you are nearing retirement or already a few years in, like me, this book helps you pause, reflect, and reimagine your next chapter with clarity and confidence.

Ramakrishna Mallimadugula,
Former Head,
India and Poland Services,
Franklin Templeton

Contents

About the Author

Hi, I am Rajesh Minocha. I am a mechanical engineer and hold an MBA in Finance from Jamnalal Bajaj Institute of Management Studies (JBIMS) in Mumbai. I was born in Dehradun and have travelled all over the country, including 21 years in South India, but now call Greater Noida home. After spending over 21 years in leadership roles at companies like ICICI, HCL Technologies, and Franklin Templeton, I retired from corporate life at the end of 2016 at the age of 45, having achieved financial freedom.

For the past decade, I have been an avid reader, diving into a variety of topics. But I have always had a special interest in personal finance, biographies, and self-help books. My passion for writing books began very recently, in 2023, when I published my first book, **Retire on your terms: A Guide to Holistic Retirement.** In the book, I share how I navigated my journey to financial independence. The book's main message is that retirement should be on your terms, not anyone else's. I talk about the non-financial side of retirement - both the ups and downs - how to know when you are ready, common mistakes people make, and more. The book is available globally on Amazon, both as a paperback and as an e-book. I urge you to buy and leave a review on Amazon.

In addition to books, I also write blogs on my website, www.financialradiance.com. Every year, in my blogs, I share my journey and perspective on my work anniversary. There have been eight so far. I also write on various personal finance topics, offering practical advice. You may want to check it out.

I like to write in a relaxed, conversational style that makes it simple for people to connect with what I want to convey. It is important to me that my writing feels relatable and useful.

The story of how I started writing is quite interesting. In my second career as a Certified Financial Planner (CFP), I interact with people all over the world. Many of them have been curious about how I managed to retire early and live a life centered around my passions. I realised that writing a book would allow me to reach a much broader audience than just through one-on-one conversations, and that is what motivated me to write my first book. It did well, and that success inspired me to start working on a sequel, focusing on life after retirement - how to find purpose, stay engaged, and create a fulfilling second career. Financial independence is great, but life can feel empty without a passion after retirement. Having enough money is not sufficient, as studies show that money is not a motivator after you have what you need.

Writing is something I do when I feel the need to reach a wider audience, but it is not my main focus. As a Certified Financial Planner (CFP), my primary goal is to help people achieve their financial dreams. Outside of work, I love travelling to off-the-beaten-path places that aren't crowded but give me a real sense of discovery and satisfaction.

Thank you so much for taking the time to read my book, Second Innings on your terms: Passionate retirement for life. I would love to stay connected with you, so feel free to share your thoughts - whether positive or critical. You can leave a review on Amazon or drop me a line.

If you would like to know more about me, then please check out my digital business card by scanning this QR code.

The first book in my series was *Retire on Your Terms – A Guide to Holistic Retirement,* published in June 2023. It was followed by the second book, ***Second Innings on Your Terms: Passionate Retirement for Life***, and the third, *Purpose Beyond Paychecks: Where Career Meets Calling*—which will be republished in 2025 as *The Career Escape Plan: From a Job You Hate to a Life You Love.* All three books are available on Amazon and other platforms globally.

If you are curious about more of my work, check out my blogs at https://www.financialradiance.com/blog, where I write periodically.

I am always open to hearing your feedback.
Email me at: contact@rajeshminocha.com
Connect on LinkedIn: Rajesh Minocha

Happy reading!

Preface

This is the second book in what has unexpectedly turned into a series. In 2023, I published my first book, **Retire on Your Terms: A Guide to Holistic Retirement**, and its success was truly humbling. I received such positive feedback that I felt encouraged to dive deeper into the non-financial aspects of retirement, which is why I decided to write this sequel.

In this book, **Second Innings on Your Terms: Passionate Retirement for Life**, I focus on the transition from working life to retirement - a time that can be exciting but also challenging. I explore the various options you can consider once you have retired to keep yourself meaningfully engaged. I believe that staying engaged during retirement is crucial, not only for our well-being but also as a way to give back to society. After I retired from corporate life at 45, I felt a strong urge to follow my passion: helping others achieve financial freedom on their own terms. That motivation is what drove me to write this second book. I want to encourage more people to pursue their passions rather than just work to pay the bills.

Writing my first book, **Retire on Your Terms**, wasn't difficult for me because I already had many ideas brewing in my mind. Over the years, in my conversations with people from all walks of life, I have heard them express their goals and dreams about achieving financial freedom. Their thoughts, combined with my own experiences, formed the basis for that book. When I wrote, I finished it in just a month because the ideas flowed so naturally.

The same was true for this book, **Second Innings on Your Terms**, too. I already knew what I wanted to say. It was just a matter of putting it all down on paper. I hope that after reading this book, you will feel inspired to take a step back and reflect on your life's goals - both financial and personal. Before diving into the post-work phase of life, it is essential to make sure your financial foundation is strong, but it is equally important to think about how you want to spend your time and energy after retiring.

One thing I loved hearing from readers of my first book was that they felt as if I were sitting right in front of them, having a conversation. I have tried to keep that same tone in this book as well - these are my thoughts, shared directly with you.

Have you read my previous book, Retire on Your Terms: A Holistic Guide to Retirement?

Well, if you read it, you probably liked it. Otherwise, you would not have purchased this book. But let me be honest. You will find a few repetitions from that book in this book. Anticipate this. The fundamental ideas stay the same, and there's no harm in getting them reinforced. Additionally, those who haven't read the previous book should grasp some key concepts to enjoy this one.

However, I am confident that you will find a lot of new concepts and food for thought in this book. This book focuses primarily on what to do after retirement, whereas the previous book provided an overview of the non-financial aspects of retirement. It included the pros and cons of early retirement, how we know that we are financially ready for retirement, and the mistakes that people make during retirement. The book also provided calculations to determine the appropriate amount of money for retirement. As mentioned earlier, this book explores retirement options.

I hope you enjoy reading this book as much as I enjoyed writing it. Whether you are still preparing for retirement or are already retired, I hope this book offers you a fresh perspective on how to view this new chapter of life.

What can you expect in the various chapters of this book?

Chapter 1, *Navigating the Transition: From Work to Play*, explores the shift from a structured work life to the open-ended nature of retirement. It offers strategies to help retirees rediscover purpose, overcome challenges like guilt or lack of direction, and create a balanced, fulfilling routine that maximizes both relaxation and personal growth in this new phase of life.

Chapter 2, *Rediscovering Passions: Finding New Pursuits*, emphasises the importance of reigniting personal passions and exploring new interests for a fulfilling, balanced life. It highlights how engaging in a activities that bring joy can reduce stress, increase happiness, and provide a sense of purpose, particularly as one approaches retirement.

Chapter 3, *Financial Freedom: Planning for a Secure Future*, outlines the importance of understanding your financial situation, setting clear goals, and building a comprehensive financial plan for a secure future. Achieving financial freedom requires thoughtful planning, disciplined saving, and regular monitoring to ensure long-term stability, especially as you approach retirement.

Chapter 4, *Health and Wellness: Maintaining a Vibrant Lifestyle*, highlights a holistic approach to well-being by focusing on balanced nutrition, regular physical activity, stress management, quality sleep, and nurturing social connections. By incorporating these practices into your daily routine, you can enhance your overall health, energy, and happiness for a fulfilling life.

Chapter 5, *Building Strong Relationships: Nurturing Connections*, emphasises the importance of trust, communication, empathy, and respect in creating meaningful relationships. By investing time and effort into building and maintaining connections, we enhance our emotional support systems, find joy, and cultivate a sense of belonging.

Chapter 6, *Giving Back: Making a Difference in Your Community*, highlights the personal and societal rewards of volunteering, emphasising how giving time, skills, or resources can improve communities while enriching one's own life. By aligning with personal passions and skills, individuals can find meaningful ways to contribute, fostering stronger connections, a sense of purpose, and a long-term positive impact on society.

Chapter 7, *Learning for Life: Continuing Education and Growth*, stresses the necessity of lifelong learning in an evolving world, helping individuals stay adaptable, informed, and personally fulfilled. By engaging in formal, informal, and experiential learning, people can expand their knowledge, enhance their career prospects, and contribute positively to society while fostering intellectual curiosity and self-growth.

Chapter 8, *Travel Adventures: Exploring New Horizons*, highlights the transformative power of adventure travel, offering a blend of physical challenges, cultural immersion, and personal growth. By stepping outside the routine and exploring new environments, travellers can push their boundaries, gain unique perspectives, and create lifelong memories.

Chapter 9, *Finding Purpose: Discovering Your Life's Mission*, explores the profound journey of uncovering a personal sense of purpose beyond mere achievements. It highlights self-reflection, aligning values with actions, and navigating challenges to create a fulfilling and meaningful life.

Chapter 10, *Embracing Serenity: Cultivating Inner Peace,* offers strategies for finding tranquillity in a fast-paced world by integrating mindfulness, nature, and healthy habits into daily life. It stresses that inner peace is an active pursuit involving mindset shifts, stress management, and meaningful relationships.

I hope I have covered all the topics relevant to this book. Please let me know if I have missed any important topics related to the second innings after retirement, and I will incorporate them into future editions.

Introduction

The book, **Second Innings on Your Terms**, is a sequel to my previous book, **Retire on Your Terms**. The book begins with the chapter titled "Navigating the Transition: From Work to Play." It challenges the conventional view of retirement as a period of relaxation and withdrawal. Instead, it presents retirement as a phase full of opportunities for growth, contribution, and fulfillment, advocating a "second career" that aligns with personal passions, values, and interests. Unlike earlier careers, driven by financial needs or societal expectations, this new phase allows retirees to explore paths that were previously inaccessible due to life obligations.

Retirement, while often liberating, can also bring feelings of loss or disconnection. A second career offers a sense of purpose, accomplishment, and structure in combating these challenges. This career doesn't have to be full-time or traditional; it can be part-time, freelance, or project-based, offering flexibility and the freedom to prioritise well-being, family, and leisure.

Work must align with personal passions, inspiring retirees to transform hobbies into businesses, engage in nonprofit endeavours, or delve into the arts. For some, a second career might also fulfill financial needs, offering strategic ways to supplement income while finding personal satisfaction. Age is an asset, not a limitation, with retirees' wealth of experience making them valuable in roles like consulting, coaching, or mentoring. Practical tips include staying updated on industry trends, acquiring new skills, and leveraging technology and networks.

Ultimately, retirement is a time of opportunity and choice, empowering retirees to embrace their second innings with optimism and create a meaningful, purpose-driven life on their terms.

1

Navigating the Transition: From Work to Play

"You have worked hard; now play harder. retiring means less work and more play."

The transition from the structured, goal-oriented world of work to the more open-ended realm of leisure is a pivotal shift that can be both exhilarating and disorienting. When we are working, our routine is more or less fixed, like getting ready for work, driving to work, working on the deliverables, attending meetings, providing leadership and direction, getting back into the traffic, coming back home, spending some time with the family, watching some television, going to sleep, and then the cycle repeats itself the next day. Upon retirement, however, one may find oneself without a fixed routine, a specific place to go, or any planned activities. It is accompanied by uncertainty and a lack of direction. After years, if not decades, of having your day dictated by work responsibilities and deadlines, the sudden expanse of free time can be overwhelming. This chapter will delve into strategies to navigate this transition effectively, helping you rediscover your passions, fill your days with purpose, and ultimately maximise your enjoyment and fulfillment in this new phase of life.

Whether you are stepping into retirement, taking an extended break, or simply seeking to reframe your approach to leisure, it is important to recognise that this adjustment does not always come naturally. Like any major life change, retirement calls for a shift in both mindset and habits. Fortunately, by embracing a few key strategies, this transition can become an opportunity to boost well-being, strengthen relationships, and pursue new paths of personal growth.

Understanding the transition

Moving from the structured confines of work to the open-ended nature of leisure involves a significant change in mindset. At work, most of us are accustomed to clearly defined tasks, deadlines, and expectations. The demands of a typical workday require focused attention, task completion, and adherence to a specific set of rules or objectives. In contrast, leisure time often invites spontaneity, creativity, and a more relaxed approach. This shift can be both liberating and, at times, unsettling.

The freedom of leisure, while freeing, can also evoke feelings of restlessness, boredom, or even guilt. Many individuals find it difficult to shed the productivity mindset they have cultivated over the years. The sudden absence of structure, routine, and purpose can leave some feeling adrift and uncertain of how to fill their time meaningfully. However, by acknowledging this discomfort and taking intentional steps to reshape how you view your free time, you can avoid falling into these common traps and instead use this period to cultivate a more balanced, enriched lifestyle.

Recognising and addressing challenges

As you transition from work to leisure, it is natural to encounter a few emotional and mental hurdles. Recognising these challenges early on will help you address them more effectively.

Guilt or obligation: For many, especially those who have spent years working in demanding roles, there is often an underlying sense of guilt during downtime. The ingrained belief that "idle hands" are unproductive can make it difficult to fully enjoy leisure without feeling the need to be constantly doing something "useful." To combat this, it is crucial to remind yourself that relaxation is not just a luxury but an essential component of a balanced life. You have earned this time, and it is important to embrace it without feeling guilty. Rest allows your mind to recharge, your body to heal, and your creativity to flourish.

Difficulty relaxing: At first, the rapid pace and constant stimulation of work can make the art of relaxation seem difficult and frustrating. If you find yourself struggling to slow down, consider adopting mindfulness practices.

Techniques like deep breathing, meditation, or even a quiet walk in nature can help ease the transition into a more relaxed state. Creating a dedicated relaxation space in your home, where you can unwind without distractions, may also help signal to your mind that it is time to shift gears.

Lack of purpose or direction: Without the daily structure and sense of accomplishment that work provides, some individuals may struggle to find meaning in their lives in their leisure time. This lack of direction can lead to feelings of dissatisfaction or even depression. To prevent this, it is essential to explore your interests, hobbies, and passions. Setting personal goals - whether big or small - can give your free time purpose. You might also consider volunteering or mentoring to use your time and skills in a way that positively impacts others, thereby adding a deeper sense of fulfillment to your leisure activities.

Strategies for a successful transition

Take advantage of this transition by planning your leisure time. Here are some key strategies to help ensure that your time off feels enriching rather than overwhelming.

Create a balanced schedule: While it is important to avoid feeling overly regimented and controlled by the clock during your free time, having some structure can be beneficial. A well-balanced schedule allows you to stay engaged without the pressures of work. Try allocating time for a variety of activities, such as hobbies, social interactions, self-care, and learning new skills. This ensures that your days remain diverse and stimulating. You can find the perfect balance between relaxation and activity by following a light, flexible routine.

Set realistic goals: Just because you are not working doesn't mean you shouldn't have a purpose. Establishing achievable goals, whether it is learning a new instrument, a new language, picking up a new hobby, or simply spending more time with family, gives you something to look forward to. These goals can also provide a sense of direction, accomplishment, and motivation. Keep in mind that these goals should be enjoyable and meaningful - there is no pressure here to "perform" as you would at work. The key is to derive joy and satisfaction from your progress, no matter how small.

Prioritise self-care: Making self-care a priority is essential for both physical and mental well-being. Whether it is engaging in regular exercise, practising meditation, or spending time outdoors, dedicating time to your health ensures that you stay energised and positive. As you move through this new phase, remember that self-care is not just about pampering yourself; it is about maintaining your health so that you can fully enjoy this new chapter in life.

Connect with others: Social connections are crucial for a fulfilling life, especially as you step away from the workplace, where many of your daily interactions might have occurred. Maintain strong relationships with family and friends, and don't be afraid to seek out new communities. Join clubs or groups that interest you, volunteer for causes you are passionate about, or engage in activities that bring you into contact with like-minded individuals. Strong social ties enhance your sense of belonging and provide support during the transition.

Explore new interests: Retirement or free time is the perfect opportunity to venture into new experiences. Don't be afraid to try things outside your comfort zone - whether it is learning a new language, travelling to unfamiliar places, or taking up a creative hobby like painting or photography. These explorations can open up new avenues for self-discovery and personal growth, adding more joy and excitement to your life.

Mindful engagement: Practicing mindfulness can help you fully savour your leisure activities.

Engaging in a hobby, spending time with loved ones, or simply relaxing, mindfulness enables you to remain present and cherish every moment. Pay attention to your surroundings, tune into your senses, and let go of distractions. This will make your leisure time feel more meaningful and enjoyable.

Limit screen time: In today's digital age, it is easy to spend hours in front of screens, whether television or mobile phones, often without realising it. While technology can be helpful, excessive screen time can lead to feelings of isolation and detachment. Set boundaries for your digital devices and prioritise face-to-face interactions or outdoor activities. Limiting screen time improves your well-being and connection to the world.

Create a relaxing environment: Your surroundings play a big role in your ability to unwind. Designate a specific space in your home as a relaxation zone - a place where you can retreat when you need a break. This space should be comfortable, inviting, and free from distractions, helping you to mentally and physically shift into a more relaxed state.

Reflect and adjust: As you navigate this new phase of life, it is important to regularly reflect on your leisure activities. If you find that something isn't working or isn't as enjoyable as you thought, don't hesitate to make adjustments. Be open to change, and permit yourself to try new things without judgment. Retirement or extended time off is about discovering what truly makes you happy, and that process will evolve.

A story about two good friends

Mr. Abhijit Arora and Mr. Surinder Singh (names changed) have been very good friends since they were in school together. Both retired about five years ago and were looking forward to the transition. Mr. Arora decided to watch television the whole day (and night), while Mr. Singh leads an active life doing his regular exercises and marathons. He also volunteers to educate young girls. Both friends' lifestyle changes impacted them very differently. Mr. Singh is always very energetic and is leading a healthy life, while Mr. Arora is getting older much faster. Mr. Arora's eyesight is rapidly deteriorating, and his lack of physical activity is negatively impacting his metabolism. Mr. Singh urges Mr. Arora to accompany him on his workouts and strolls, yet Mr. Arora wants to maintain his current lifestyle, believing that this is what society expects from those who retire.

Key Takeaways:

- Navigating the transition from work to leisure requires conscious effort, patience, and self-awareness.
- We need to let go of old habits and embrace new possibilities.
- By understanding and implementing effective strategies, we can create a fulfilling, enjoyable, and meaningful life outside of work.
- The goal is not to eliminate work entirely from your life but rather to find a healthy balance that promotes both productivity and well-being.
- With a little planning and the right mindset, the transition into leisure can be one of the most rewarding experiences of your life.

2
Rediscovering Passions: Finding New Pursuits

"Working hard for something we don't care about is called stress: Working hard for something we love is called passion." – Simon Sinek

We often lose sight of the things that genuinely offer us joy in the daily grind of today's fast-paced world. Our work lives often consume a significant portion of our time, leaving little time for personal pursuits. Over time, this constant focus on productivity can lead to burnout, stress, and a feeling of emptiness. However, rediscovering our passions and finding new avenues for enjoyment is essential for a fulfilling and balanced life. These passions are not just hobbies, but they contribute significantly to our overall well-being and sense of purpose. This chapter explores the importance of stepping away from work, carving out time for ourselves, and exploring new hobbies and interests. Through this process, we learn that life is about more than just meeting deadlines. It is about finding meaning and joy in the moments in between.

You may wonder about the appropriateness of this chapter in this book since this book focusses on life after retirement. It is crucial to focus on your passions even before retirement, while you are still working, to ensure a smooth transition. We get so absorbed in our regular work that we often don't even know what our passion is or what makes us happy. Exploring a few options while working will help us zero in on what makes us truly fulfilled. We must initiate this process of finding our passion at least five years before the planned retirement. Furthermore, once we secure employment, it becomes significantly simpler to form and sustain relationships with individuals who share our passions or who can serve as mentors to assist us in advancing our passions.

Passions are important

Passions are deeply rooted interests that bring us a sense of purpose, fulfillment, and enjoyment. They can range from creative pursuits like painting or writing to physical activities like hiking or dancing. Engaging in activities we love can benefit our mental, emotional, and physical well-being. When we invest time in things that excite us, we experience a renewed sense of energy and enthusiasm that positively influences all aspects of our lives.

Stress reduction: Engaging in hobbies can help alleviate stress and anxiety by providing a mental escape from the pressures of work and daily life. When we are fully immersed in something we enjoy, our minds naturally shift away from our worries, allowing us to relax and recharge.

Increased happiness: Pursuing our passions can boost our mood and overall happiness. When we do things we enjoy, we release feel-good chemicals like dopamine and serotonin. These natural mood enhancers can improve our emotional health and contribute to a more positive outlook on life.

Enhanced creativity: Engaging in creative activities can stimulate our imagination and problem-solving skills. Creative pursuits, whether they involve brainstorming ideas for a project or thinking creatively in daily life, enhance our ability to approach challenges with fresh perspectives.

Improved self-esteem: Accomplishing goals and mastering new skills can boost our self-confidence and self-esteem. As we see tangible progress in areas we are passionate about, we develop a stronger sense of self-worth and capability.

Better relationships: Shared passions can help us connect with like-minded people and build stronger relationships. Whether through joining clubs, attending workshops, or simply talking with others about mutual interests, passions can serve as a bridge that brings people together in meaningful ways.

Finding new passions

If you are struggling to identify your passions, don't worry. Many people feel disconnected from their interests at some point in life, especially after years of focussing solely on work or responsibilities. The positive news is that it is never too late to rediscover old passions or uncover new ones. Here are some strategies to help you rediscover or discover new passions:

Reflect on childhood interests: Think back to the activities you enjoyed as a child. Were you drawn to art, music, sports, or nature? These early interests may provide clues to your current passions. Sometimes, revisiting the things that once brought us joy can reignite our enthusiasm in surprising ways.

Discover new experiences: Try new activities and venture outside of your comfort zone. Take a class, volunteer, or travel to a new destination. New experiences often lead to new passions. You may discover hidden talents or interests you never knew you had. Allow yourself to experiment without the pressure of perfection - exploration is part of the process.

Pay attention to your emotions: Notice the activities that make you feel energised, excited, or fulfilled. These may be indicators of your passions. When you find yourself looking forward to something or feeling a sense of accomplishment afterward, that is a clear sign you are on the right track.

Consider your values: What is important to you in life? Are you passionate about making a difference in the world, learning new things, or connecting with others?

Your values can guide you toward meaningful pursuits. For example, if you value community service, volunteering may become a source of fulfillment and joy.

Talk to others: Discuss your interests with friends, family, or mentors. They may have insights or suggestions that can help you explore new possibilities. Sometimes, an outside perspective can help us see what we may have overlooked, and their enthusiasm for their passions might inspire us to try something new.

Balancing work and play

Finding time for personal pursuits can be challenging, especially if you have a demanding job or family obligations. However, it is important to prioritise your passions and make time for them. Allowing ourselves the freedom to engage in activities we love is not a luxury but a necessity for our overall well-being. Furthermore, because this book focuses on life after retirement, we read it primarily during our working years to better understand our passions. There will be enough time to follow the passion during retirement. Therefore, we should not overdo it, as that can impact our present responsibilities, which can even jeopardise our plan for retirement at the age we had envisaged. Therefore, we must delicately strike a balance.

Here are some tips for balancing work and play:

Set boundaries: Establish clear boundaries between work and personal time. Avoid checking work emails or taking calls outside of work hours. By creating a clear distinction between work and personal life, you will make space for the things that bring you joy without feeling guilty or distracted. After the pandemic, the work-life situation has made it even more difficult to find the line between office and home, but we still need to set boundaries.

Create a schedule: Plan time for your hobbies and interests in your weekly schedule. Treat your passions like important appointments. Committing time to your interests, whether it's an hour of reading before bed or a weekend hiking trip, ensures that other obligations don't sideline them.

Find a support system: Surround yourself with people who support your interests and encourage you to pursue your passions. A strong support system can make a world of difference, providing motivation and encouragement when life gets busy.

Start small: Don't feel pressured to dive into a new hobby with a big-bang approach. Start small and gradually increase your involvement. This allows you to test the waters and build momentum without feeling overwhelmed.

Be flexible: Life can be unpredictable. Prepare to adjust your plans and be flexible with your hobbies.

The goal is to integrate your passions into your life in a sustainable way, not to create additional stress by trying to stick to a rigid plan.

Be aware of passion. Do not go overboard

Mr. Ayub Khan is passionate about travelling the world. He was keenly awaiting his retirement, as he could not follow his passion due to his hectic work schedule. As soon as he retired, he wanted to complete his bucket list at the earliest, knowing the risk of not being able to travel so much after he got old. Unfortunately, within the first three years of retirement, he depleted a significant portion of his retirement corpus. He now understands the impact and realises that he will need to either return to work and earn money or reduce his lifestyle, both of which he finds unacceptable.

———————∞———————

Key Takeaways

- Rediscovering our passions and finding new pursuits is essential for a fulfilling and balanced life.
- We should evaluate and ignite our passions during our working lives, not wait until retirement.
- By exploring our interests and engaging in activities we love, we can reduce stress, increase happiness, enhance creativity, improve self-esteem, and build stronger relationships.

- The things that ignite our passions offer beauty, joy, and meaning. So, take the time to explore what brings you joy, embrace the journey of self-discovery, and make it a priority in your life.
- The rewards will not only enhance your happiness but will ripple out into every other aspect of your life, from a fulfilled retirement to happy relationships.

3

Financial Freedom:
Planning for a Secure Future

"As in all successful ventures, the foundation of a good retirement is planning." – Earl Nightingale

Financial freedom means being able to live your life without worrying about money. It is the ability to live your life without constantly worrying about money. It represents a state where you are not only able to cover your basic needs and wants but also have the financial flexibility to pursue your dreams and goals without stress. Financial freedom is about choice. Financial limitations do not constrain you from making decisions that align with your values and desires. Achieving this goal is something that many people strive for, but it requires planning, discipline, and a clear understanding of the financial picture. This chapter will serve as a roadmap to financial freedom, outlining the steps you can take to better understand your current financial situation, set achievable goals, and build a financial plan that will help you secure your future.

Before deciding to hang up the boots, you should take this crucial step. Once completed, this step will be extremely difficult to recover from, and if done improperly, it could potentially negatively impact personal relationships at home. This is a step that applies even to those entering retirement. They must periodically evaluate whether their corpus will continue to sustain itself as per the assumptions. There may be other changes in personal circumstances that necessitate adjustments to the numbers. We should never overlook the impact of inflation and the rise in life expectancy levels, which are both important considerations. A deteriorating health status could also mean a greater need for money during retirement, so it is important to keep an additional buffer when calculating the retirement corpus.

Understanding your financial situation

To attain financial freedom, you must first have a thorough awareness of your existing financial circumstances. A comprehensive image of your earnings, expenses, debts, and assets is part of this. It can be challenging to create realistic goals and make well-informed judgements without this basis. Start by gathering information about your monthly income, whether it is from a salary, freelance work, or investments. Then, take an honest look at your expenses - both essential, like rent and groceries, and non-essential, like entertainment or dining out.

Additionally, assessing your debts is critical. This covers any outstanding balances you owe on your credit card, personal loans, student loans, and other debts. Understanding the interest rates, minimum payments, and total amounts of each debt will allow you to prioritise repayment strategies effectively. Finally, calculate your total assets, including savings, retirement accounts, investments, and property. Knowing where you stand financially is empowering, as it sets the stage for proactive steps toward financial freedom. The final step is to calculate your cash net worth, which is the sum of your assets minus your liabilities minus the value of the house you contemplate retiring in.

This was covered in details in my first book, **Retire on your terms**. Chapter 15. We discussed how to calculate how much you need for your retirement. Grab your  copy on Amazon if you need to know this. Please scan this QR code.

Setting financial objectives

The next step is to define specific financial goals after you have a thorough picture of your money. Your goals should follow the SMART framework, meaning they should be Specific, Measurable, Achievable, Relevant, and Time-bound. These goals provide a sense of direction and purpose in your financial journey and help you stay motivated along the way. Common financial goals include:

Paying off debt: This may involve credit cards, student

loans, or any other high-interest debt.

Saving for a down payment on a house: Homeownership is often a significant milestone in financial freedom.

Saving for retirement: Building a retirement fund early on helps ensure long-term financial security.

Funding your child's education: Whether through a college savings plan or another investment vehicle, planning for education expenses is a common priority.

Building an emergency fund: This fund acts as a safety net for unexpected financial emergencies, such as medical bills or job loss.

Starting a business: Entrepreneurship can be a path to financial independence, but it requires careful planning and capital.

Each of these goals should be realistic based on your current financial situation and future income potential. For instance, if paying off debt is your primary goal, focus on setting a timeline for becoming debt-free, whether in 3, 5, or 10 years, depending on your situation.

Developing a financial plan

Once you have set your financial goals, it is time to develop a plan to achieve them. Your financial plan should cover several key areas, including budgeting, debt repayment, savings, investing, and insurance. Each of these components plays a critical role in building a strong financial foundation.

Budgeting: A budget is one of the most powerful tools for managing your finances and achieving your financial goals. You can keep track of your earnings and expenses by creating a budget, ensuring that you are living within your means. There are other approaches to budgeting, such as the 50/30/20 rule, which divides money into three categories: needs, wants, and 20% to savings, or zero-based budgeting, which allocates every dollar to a specific expense. The key is to find a method that works for you, allowing you to regularly save for your goals while covering your essential expenses.

Debt repayment: If you have debt, developing a repayment strategy should be a priority. High-interest debt can severely hinder your ability to save and build wealth. The debt snowball and debt avalanche are two common methods for debt repayment. The "debt snowball" method focuses on paying off the smallest debt first, giving you psychological wins and momentum as you move on to larger debts. The "debt avalanche" method, on the other hand, focuses on paying off debts with the highest interest rates first, saving you more money over time. Both strategies can be effective. You should pick one that suits your needs and budget.

Saving and investing: These are essential components of achieving financial freedom. Start saving for your goals as early as possible, as the power of compounding helps big time over a long time, boosting your wealth. An emergency fund should be one of your first savings goals, with a recommended balance of six months of living expenses. After building an emergency fund, you can focus on other savings goals, such as retirement, home ownership, or starting a business.

Investing allows your money to grow over time, but it is important to choose investment options that align with your risk tolerance and time horizon. For long-term goals like retirement, stocks, bonds, and mutual funds are common investment options. If you are new to investing or are very busy professionally, consider speaking with personal finance professionals for guidance.

Insurance: Often overlooked, it is a crucial aspect of financial planning. It helps protect you from unexpected events that could otherwise lead to financial ruin. Types of insurance to consider include life insurance, health insurance, auto insurance, and homeowners' or renters' insurance. Having the appropriate coverage can provide peace of mind and protect your assets in the event of illness, accidents, or other unforeseen circumstances.

Monitoring and adjusting your plan

Your financial plan is not static. It should evolve as

your life and financial circumstances change.

Regularly monitoring your progress is crucial for staying on track. At least once a year, review your budget, savings, debt, and investments to ensure that you are meeting your financial goals. If you undergo life changes like getting married, having a child, or changing jobs, you might need to make adjustments. Seeking professional help

If you feel overwhelmed by managing your finances on your own or are very busy on your professional front and cannot devote time, seeking professional help from a Certified Financial Planner (CFP) can be incredibly beneficial. A professional can help you create a personalised financial plan, provide investment advice based on your suitability, risk appetite, and time horizon, and help protect your assets. They can also offer an objective perspective and help you avoid common financial pitfalls.

A very disheartening story

Mr. Ramamoorthy (name changed) is 50 years old and is very worried. He believes his skill sets don't match market expectations, and he fears losing his job to those 15 years younger than him. He works in the finance department for a midsize company and has not improved his skills to stay up to date on key market trends. Worse, he did not do any financial planning and just splurged the money he earned to show off to his neighbours and relatives. He still has five years left on his home loan. Whatever little savings he had, he used to send his only daughter abroad for education. In an unfortunate accident, his daughter passed away. Mr. Ramamoorthy's health has prevented him from keeping up. He has no life insurance and very little savings. He is awake most nights, thinking about his wife's future if he were to pass away, considering his deteriorating health conditions.

———————∞———————

Key Takeaways

- Achieving financial freedom is a long-term goal that requires thoughtful planning, discipline, and perseverance.
- Understanding your financial situation, setting specific goals, and developing a solid financial plan will allow you to control your finances and build a secure future for yourself and your family.
- The journey to financial independence is not without challenges, but with the right tools and mindset, it is a goal that is well within reach.

Bonus ideas!

To further strengthen your path to financial freedom, here are some additional tips to keep in mind:

- **Live below your means:** This entails spending less than you earn and resisting the temptation to overspend.
- **Automate your savings:** To make sure you are constantly saving, set up automatic transfers from

your checking account to your investment or savings accounts.

- **Invest for the long term:** Avoid trying to time the market; instead, focus on steady, long- term growth.
- **Get educated about personal finance:** read books, attend seminars, or consult financial advisors to increase your knowledge and confidence. Not being from a financial background is not an excuse. Additionally, it's in your best interest to monitor your money.
- **Be patient:** Building wealth takes time. Stick to your plan, and the results will follow over time.

4

Health and Wellness: Maintaining a Vibrant Lifestyle

"If you don't make time for exercise, you'll probably have to make time for illness." – Robin Sharma

Health and wellness are the cornerstones of a fulfilling and vibrant life. They encompass not only physical well-being but also the interconnected mental, emotional, and social dimensions. By making health a priority, you can not only improve your overall quality of life but also boost your energy levels, enhance your productivity, and significantly reduce your risk of chronic diseases like heart disease, diabetes, and mental health disorders. However, achieving optimal wellness involves more than just occasional healthy habits. In this chapter, we will explore these key strategies in-depth, providing you with the tools and insights to create a balanced and sustainable healthy lifestyle that nourishes both your body and mind.

Nutrition: Fueling your body

Nutrition is the foundation of optimal health. Your diet can either provide your body with the nutrients it needs or deprive it of vital nutrients. You can keep your energy levels up, your immune system strong, and your digestive system running smoothly by eating a varied and balanced diet that is high in fresh produce, whole grains, lean meats, healthy fats, and other nutrients.

Hydration: Water is crucial for almost every bodily function, from maintaining proper body temperature to aiding in digestion and nutrient absorption. Aim for at least eight glasses of water a day, but remember that individual hydration needs can vary based on activity level, climate, and personal health. You can also include hydrating foods like cucumbers, watermelon, and oranges in your diet.

Portion control: Managing portion sizes is key to avoiding overeating, which can lead to weight gain and digestive issues. By using smaller plates, practicing mindful eating, and paying attention to hunger cues, you can keep your portion sizes in check while still enjoying a variety of foods.

Limit processed foods: Processed foods often contain unhealthy fats, excess sodium, and added sugars, which can lead to various health issues, such as obesity, heart disease, and high blood pressure. Prioritising whole foods over processed alternatives ensures that you are getting the highest quality nutrients without harmful additives.

Mindful eating: In today's fast-paced world, eating often becomes a rushed activity. By practising mindful eating - slowing down and paying attention to flavours and textures - your body signals hunger and fullness. You can then foster a healthier relationship with food. This not only improves digestion but also helps to prevent overeating and enhances your overall enjoyment of meals.

Physical activity: Moving your body

Regular exercise is critical for both mental and physical well-being. It helps to maintain a healthy weight, improve cardiovascular fitness, strengthen muscles and bones, and boost your mood by releasing endorphins - the body's natural "feel-good" chemicals. Regular movement can also lower your risk for chronic diseases such as heart disease, diabetes, and certain cancers.

Find activities you enjoy: Sustainability is key when it comes to exercise. Finding physical activities that you genuinely enjoy will increase the likelihood that you stick with them in the long term. Whether it is walking in nature, dancing, yoga, or swimming, choose activities that make you feel positive and fit your lifestyle.

Incorporate strength training: While cardio is beneficial for heart health, strength training is essential for building and maintaining muscle mass, which naturally declines as we age. Incorporating bodyweight exercises, resistance bands, or weights into your routine two to three times a week can help improve muscle tone, increase metabolism, and boost bone density, reducing the risk of osteoporosis.

Stay active throughout the day: Even if you have a regular exercise routine, it is important to stay engaged throughout the day, especially if you have a sedentary job. Simple actions like taking short walking breaks, standing while working, or using the stairs instead of the elevator can add up to significantly improve your daily physical activity levels.

Stress management: Nurturing your mind

Stress is an inevitable consequence of living in today's fast-paced society. But worry, despair, heart disease, and gastrointestinal disorders are just some of the physical and mental health problems that can worsen with prolonged exposure to stress. For long-term health, it is crucial to find ways to handle stress. Stress management techniques that emphasise mindfulness include deep breathing exercises and meditation. These methods are great for reducing anxiety, sharpening concentration, and establishing a state of tranquillity within. As little as a few minutes of daily mindfulness practice can greatly improve your ability to handle stress.

Time management: For many people, poor time management is a major source of stress. By learning to prioritise tasks, delegate when necessary, and break larger projects into smaller, manageable steps, you can reduce feelings of being overwhelmed and maintain better control over your schedule.

Relaxation techniques: Yoga, Tai Chi, or progressive muscle relaxation are all excellent ways to calm the body and mind when practiced regularly. Relaxation, reduced muscular tension, and increased flexibility are all benefits of these stress-busting routines. These practices promote relaxation, reduce muscle tension, and improve flexibility, all while helping to combat stress.

Social support: Never underestimate the importance of a support network when managing stress. Talking through your concerns with friends, family, or a professional can provide valuable perspective, help you process emotions, and alleviate feelings of isolation.

Sleep: Prioritising rest

Often overlooked as a crucial component of health, adequate sleep is essential to your health and wellness. Mental clarity, emotional stability, immune system support, and physical recuperation all depend on a healthy night's sleep.

Create a sleep-conducive environment: To optimise sleep, your bedroom should be a restful sanctuary. Keep the room dark, quiet, and cool to promote better sleep. Consider using blackout curtains, white noise machines, or a fan to create a more sleep-friendly environment.

Establish a consistent sleep schedule: Even on weekends, sticking to a regular bedtime and wake time will assist your body's internal clock balance, making it easier to fall asleep and allowing you to wake up feeling refreshed.

Limit screen time before bed: The blue light emitted by phones, tablets, and computers can interfere with your body's production of melatonin, a hormone that helps regulate sleep. To improve sleep quality, try to avoid screens at least an hour before bed.

Avoid stimulants before bed: Caffeine and alcohol can disrupt sleep, so it is best to limit their consumption, especially in the evening. Instead, opt for a calming bedtime routine that promotes relaxation, such as reading or taking a warm bath.

Social connections: Building relationships

The mental and emotional well-being of an individual depends on the strength of their social ties since humans are fundamentally sociable. Aside from the obvious psychological and physiological benefits, such as decreased stress and improved immune function, having supportive relationships helps alleviate feelings of isolation and loneliness.

Spend time with loved ones: Regular interaction with close friends and family members strengthens bonds and provides emotional nourishment. Make it a priority to carve out time for meaningful conversations and activities with the people who matter most to you.

Join social groups or clubs: Engaging in group activities centred around shared interests, such as book clubs, sports teams, or hobby groups. It can help you meet new people and foster a sense of belonging.

Volunteer: Volunteering not only benefits your community but also provides you with a sense of purpose and fulfillment. Helping others can boost your mood and broaden your social circle by connecting you with like-minded individuals.

Online communities offer another avenue for building social connections in today's digital age. Whether through social media, forums, or interest-based groups, these platforms can provide valuable support and camaraderie, especially if in-person interaction is limited.

Building social connections with wellness

Understanding the value of social connections, Mr. John Gonsalves, 65 years old, who retired 7 years ago, began organising weekly coffee meetups with friends. These gatherings became a supportive and comfortable environment for sharing, bonding, and enjoying one another's company. This initiative deepened his friendships and offered a reliable source of emotional support and renewal. This story shows how simple practices - whether through mindfulness, creativity, setting boundaries, physical activity, or fostering social ties can greatly enhance emotional well-being, demonstrating the many ways retirees can take charge of their mental health.

———————∞———————

Key Takeaways

- Achieving and maintaining a vibrant lifestyle is about more than just a quick fix. It is about adopting a holistic approach that nurtures your physical, mental, emotional, and social well-being.
- By incorporating balanced nutrition, regular physical activity, effective stress management, quality sleep, and strong social connections into your daily life, you can significantly improve your overall health and happiness.
- The key to lasting wellness lies in making small, sustainable changes that gradually transform your lifestyle, helping you feel more energised, focussed, and fulfilled.

5

Building Strong Relationships: Nurturing Connections

"The meeting of two personalities is like the contact of two chemical substances: if there is any reaction, both are transformed." - Carl Jung

Relationships form the foundation of our lives, shaping who we are and how we experience the world around us. Whether with family, friends, romantic partners, or colleagues, these connections are essential for emotional support, companionship, and a sense of belonging. Healthy relationships can uplift us, providing joy and stability, while strained relationships can contribute to stress and dissatisfaction. This chapter delves into the importance of relationships, offering practical strategies for building, maintaining, and deepening meaningful connections that enhance not only our well-being but also the well-being of those we care about.

Understanding the importance of relationships

Relationships are crucial to both our mental and physical health. Numerous studies show that people with strong social connections tend to be happier, experience fewer mental health issues, and live longer, healthier lives. Social connections are just as important to health as diet and exercise. Individuals who enjoy close, supportive relationships are less likely to experience depression, anxiety, or loneliness. Strong relationships also act as a buffer during challenging times, offering comfort, encouragement, and a sense of security.

Moreover, meaningful relationships contribute to a greater sense of purpose. They provide opportunities for growth, collaboration, and learning, helping us navigate life's ups and downs with resilience and perspective. They engage in activities such as sharing laughter or leaning on someone during a crisis; relationships shape our narratives and help us find meaning in our experiences.

Building strong foundations

Trust, communication, empathy, and respect form the solid foundation of strong relationships. These qualities are the cornerstones of any meaningful connection, ensuring that the relationship is healthy, supportive, and fulfilling for both parties.

Trust: Trust is the glue that holds relationships together. Consistent honesty, transparency, and reliability cultivate trust. Trust allows individuals to feel secure in their relationships, knowing they can rely on each other. Building trust takes time and effort, but once established, it strengthens the bond between people and helps them weather challenges with greater confidence.

Open communication: It is the key to understanding one another. It involves more than just talking. It requires active listening, empathy, and clarity. When people feel heard and understood, they are more likely to share openly. Effective communication also involves addressing misunderstandings or conflicts early rather than letting them fester. This openness fosters mutual respect and prevents small issues from becoming larger problems.

Empathy: Empathy allows us to connect on a deeper level by understanding and sharing the feelings of others. It involves putting ourselves in someone else's shoes and offering support, even when we may not fully understand their perspective. Empathy strengthens relationships by fostering emotional intimacy and trust, allowing individuals to feel valued and understood.

Respect: Respect in relationships means acknowledging and valuing each other's differences. Everyone has unique perspectives, experiences, and feelings, and maintaining respect even in disagreements ensures that both parties feel valued. Respect also involves honouring each other's boundaries, space, and autonomy, fostering an environment of mutual regard and understanding.

Shared interests: Having shared interests can bring people closer together by providing common ground for enjoyment and connection. Whether it is a hobby, a shared passion for a cause, or simply spending time together, engaging in activities, both parties enjoy strengthening bonds and creating lasting memories.

Nurturing Existing Relationships

Relationships require regular nurturing to thrive once they establish a strong foundation. Just like a plant, relationships require attention, care, and effort to grow and sustain.

Quality time: Carving out time to spend with loved ones is essential. Work, technology, or other commitments can easily distract us in today's fast-paced world. However, dedicating focussed, undivided attention to those we care about is key to maintaining closeness. Whether it is a simple meal together or a weekend getaway, prioritising time with others fosters deeper connections.

Active listening: Genuine listening goes beyond simply hearing words. It involves being present and engaged in the conversation. To demonstrate your full understanding of the other person's thoughts and feelings, actively listen by maintaining eye contact, nodding, and responding appropriately. This helps individuals feel understood and valued.

Support and encouragement: Offering emotional support

during difficult times and celebrating achievements strengthens bonds. Being there for someone - whether they are experiencing joy or hardship. It reinforces the idea that the relationship is a safe, dependable space. Even small gestures of encouragement can go a long way in showing care.

Any relationship will inevitably encounter conflicts, but how we handle them can make a significant difference. Healthy conflict resolution involves open communication, compromise, and patience. Rather than placing blame, focus on understanding the other person's perspective and finding a solution that works for both parties. Learning to navigate disagreements constructively strengthens relationships and builds trust.

Express gratitude: Regularly expressing gratitude enhances relationships by reminding both parties of the value they bring to each other's lives. Simple acts of kindness or a heartfelt "thank you" can deepen emotional bonds and remind us to appreciate the positive aspects of our relationships.

Building new relationships

Building new relationships can be exciting yet challenging, especially as adults. It often requires stepping out of your comfort zone, but with effort and authenticity, it is possible to form meaningful connections.

Expand your social circle: Attend social events, join clubs, participate in community activities, or volunteer. These activities provide opportunities to meet new people with similar interests, making it easier to form connections. Engaging in group activities also allows relationships to develop naturally over time.

Be yourself: Authenticity is the key to building genuine relationships. People are more likely to connect with you if they believe you are true to yourself. Don't try to fit into a mould to gain approval. Let your unique personality shine through.

Be approachable: Body language plays a significant role in how others perceive you. Smile, make eye contact, and adopt an open posture to signal that you are friendly and welcoming. Being approachable invites others to initiate conversations and strengthens the likelihood of forming connections.

Initiate conversations: Don't be afraid to take the first step in starting a conversation. Asking open-ended questions and showing a genuine interest in the other person helps to build rapport. By actively engaging in the conversation, you demonstrate that you value the interaction.

Follow up: After meeting someone new, it is important to follow up to maintain the connection. Whether it is sending a quick message or arranging a coffee meet-up, taking the initiative to keep in touch shows that you are interested in building a relationship.

Overcoming Challenges

Even the strongest relationships face challenges. Learning to navigate these obstacles with patience and understanding can help preserve and strengthen your connections.

Handling conflict: Address conflicts promptly and respectfully. Rather than blaming or making accusations, focus on finding solutions together. Open communication, empathy, and compromise are key to resolving disagreements healthily and productively.

Managing expectations: Unrealistic expectations can put undue pressure on relationships. It is essential to set realistic goals and communicate openly about what you need from each other. By managing expectations, you can avoid disappointment and foster more balanced, fulfilling connections.

Handling jealousy: It is a normal emotion but can become destructive if not managed properly. Address feelings of jealousy with honesty and openness. Discuss any underlying insecurities and work together to build trust and security in the relationship.

Forgiving and moving on: Holding onto grudges can cause resentment and damage relationships over time. Learning to forgive is essential for moving forward and maintaining strong connections. Forgiveness doesn't mean forgetting, but rather letting go of the past and working toward healing and reconciliation.

Key Takeaways

- Building and nurturing strong relationships takes time, effort, and commitment.
- Whether you are fostering existing bonds or forming new connections, the principles of trust, communication, empathy, and respect are at the core of meaningful relationships.
- By applying the strategies outlined in this chapter, you can cultivate relationships that enrich your life, provide emotional support, and offer a sense of purpose and fulfillment.
- Relationships are a journey; like any worthwhile endeavour, they require patience, dedication, and care.

6
Giving Back: Making a Difference in Your Community

"The purpose of life is not to be happy. It is to be useful, to be honourable, to be compassionate, to have it make some difference that youhave lived and lived well." - Ralph Waldo Emerson

In today's fast-paced world, it is simple to become absorbed in our responsibilities and overlook the larger communities around us. Yet, giving back is not just a civic duty but also a deeply enriching and fulfilling experience that benefits both individuals and society as a whole. Whether through volunteering your time, donating resources, or offering expertise, contributing to your community helps to create a more equitable, supportive, and inclusive environment. This chapter will examine various ways to give back, explore the personal and societal benefits of volunteering, and offer guidance on how to find the volunteer opportunity that's right for you.

Embracing the spirit of giving back empowers individuals to transform their communities, positively influence the lives of others, and ultimately discover a deeper sense of purpose and connection.

The importance of giving back

The act of giving back to your community is far-reaching, with effects that extend beyond the immediate outcomes. First and foremost, it directly improves the lives of others. When you choose to volunteer - whether it is serving meals at a shelter, helping children with their education, or spending time with the elderly, you offer meaningful support that can leave a lasting and positive impact. These actions can bring relief to families facing hardship, help individuals overcome obstacles, and create opportunities for those who may not otherwise have access to support.

Furthermore, giving back can be immensely rewarding on a personal level. It can instill a sense of purpose and satisfaction that comes from contributing to a cause larger than yourself. Many people find that volunteering offers emotional benefits, such as reduced stress, improved mood, and a greater sense of accomplishment. By stepping outside of your daily routine and focussing on the needs of others, you gain perspective on life's challenges and cultivate gratitude for what you have.

On a larger scale, giving back fosters stronger, more resilient communities. When people unite to address common issues - be it poverty, environmental conservation, or education, it creates a spirit of

This collective effort can help solve local problems, increase civic engagement, and promote social inclusion. Communities thrive when individuals come together with a common purpose, and the ripple effect of these efforts can lead to long-term positive change.

Finding the right volunteer opportunity

Finding the right volunteer opportunity is essential to making your experience both meaningful and enjoyable. Volunteering should align with your passions, skills, and values so that your contributions feel meaningful. Here are some steps to help you identify the best volunteer opportunities for you:

Identify your passions: Consider the causes or issues that resonate with you on a personal level. Are you passionate about education, environmental sustainability, social justice, or animal welfare? Understanding what drives you will make the volunteer experience more fulfilling and help you stay motivated over time.

Assess your skills: Take stock of the skills and talents you possess that could benefit a volunteer organisation. For example, if you are skilled in fundraising, organising events, or offering technical support, you can leverage these abilities to contribute in a significant way. Volunteering doesn't always have to involve direct service. Many organisations need help behind the scenes in areas like marketing, grant writing, or administrative work.

Research local organisations: Likely, many local organisations are actively working on causes that matter to you. You can search online databases, contact community centres, or get in touch with local nonprofits, schools, or your town's Chamber of Commerce to explore volunteer options. Various online platforms can also help you find specific opportunities based on your interests and location.

Start small: If you are new to volunteering, it is wise to begin with a small commitment. This allows you to test the waters without feeling overwhelmed. More involvement and responsibility are possible as you gain confidence.

Ask questions: Don't hesitate to ask the organisation for more information if you are unsure about a particular opportunity. Understanding the time commitment, responsibilities, and expectations beforehand will help ensure that the role is a suitable fit for you.

Types of volunteer opportunities

There are countless ways to give back to your community, ranging from hands-on service to more behind-the-scenes support. Here are some common types of volunteer opportunities to consider:

Nonprofit organisations: Nonprofits often rely heavily on volunteers to fulfill their missions. You could assist with fundraising, provide administrative support, or help organise events. Many nonprofits also need volunteers to work directly with clients, providing services such as tutoring, mentoring, or advocacy.

Schools and universities: Educational institutions frequently seek volunteers to assist with programs like tutoring, mentoring, after-school activities, or career coaching. If you have expertise in a particular subject, you could also offer workshops or help students prepare for exams.

Hospitals and nursing homes: Many healthcare facilities rely on volunteers to provide companionship, support, and comfort to patients. Whether it's visiting patients, assisting with recreational activities, or helping with administrative tasks, your time can make a significant difference in the lives of patients and their families.

Environmental organisations: If you are passionate about the planet, consider volunteering for an environmental organisation. These groups often need help with activities like tree planting, beach cleanups, wildlife conservation, or educational outreach programs aimed at promoting sustainability.

Animal shelters: Animal lovers can volunteer at local shelters to care for animals, assist with adoption events, or help raise awareness and funds for shelter operations. Your contribution can improve the lives of animals and help families find loving, furry companions.

The benefits of volunteering

Volunteering offers a multitude of benefits, both for the community and for the individuals who give their time and energy:

Research has shown that volunteering can improve mental health by reducing stress, combating depression, and promoting emotional well-being. By focusing on helping others, volunteers often experience a sense of fulfillment that improves their overall mental health.

Increased social connection: Volunteering can help you meet new people, forge meaningful relationships, and expand your social network. It is a wonderful way to connect with like-minded individuals who share your passion for giving back.

Enhanced job prospects: Many volunteer roles help develop skills that can be beneficial in the workplace, such as leadership, project management, communication, and teamwork. Volunteer experience on a resume can also make you more appealing to employers, but retirees may not be relevant unless they plan to work full-time in this field after retirement.

Sense of purpose: Volunteering allows you to contribute to a cause you care about, which can instill a greater sense of purpose and meaning in your life.

Positive impact on the community: By giving your time

and energy, you directly contribute to the well-being of your community. Whether it is feeding the hungry, helping a child learn to read, or advocating for environmental protection, your actions create real and lasting change.

Tips for effective volunteering

To maximise your volunteer experience, have the right mindset and attitude:

Be reliable: Once you commit to a volunteer role, ensure that you follow through. Organisations depend on their volunteers, so showing up on time and being dependable is crucial.

Be enthusiastic: Approach your volunteer work with a positive attitude. Contagious excitement can motivate others to be enthusiastic.

Be respectful: Treat everyone with kindness and respect, from the people you're helping to your fellow volunteers and the organisation's staff. A respectful attitude fosters a collaborative and supportive environment.

Be flexible: Volunteering can sometimes involve unexpected changes or challenges. Adaptability and willingness to accept new tasks or shifts in responsibilities will make you a more valuable volunteer.

Be grateful: Finally, express gratitude for the opportunity to volunteer. Whether it's thanking the organisation for allowing you to contribute or showing appreciation to the people you serve, gratitude helps foster a positive experience for everyone involved.

Story: Mentoring inner-city youth

Heather Monahan's mother left her father with no job and four children to support, forcing them to live in an abandoned trailer behind her grandparents' house in Worcester, Massachusetts. Despite hardships, her mother worked three jobs to provide for the family. Monahan eventually rose above her difficult upbringing to become a media executive in South Beach, Florida. She currently serves on the board of City Year Miami, mentors' women in business, and has received recognition for her ability to overcome adversity, including her successful recovery from divorce as a "boss in heels". (Source: Reader's Digest).

Key takeaways

- Serving your community is a powerful way to improve the world and your life.
- Whether you are passionate about helping children, protecting the environment, caring for animals, or supporting those in need, there is a volunteer opportunity that's right for you.
- Volunteering offers not only a chance to contribute to meaningful causes but also personal benefits such as

increased well-being, new friendships, and valuable skills.

- By finding a cause that speaks to your heart and dedicating your time and energy, you can help create a more positive, equitable, and connected society.

7
Learning for Life: Continuing Education and Growth

"Anyone who stops learning is old, whether at twenty or eighty. Anyone who keeps learning stays young. The greatest thing in life is to keep your mind young." -
Henry Ford

In today's rapidly evolving world, the concept of lifelong learning has taken on greater importance than ever before. With constant advances in technology, shifts in industries, and changes in societal expectations, staying informed and adaptable is no longer a luxury - it is a necessity. Lifelong learning goes beyond the formal education we receive in schools or universities. It is an ongoing process of acquiring new knowledge, skills, and perspectives throughout one's life. This chapter explores the significance of continuous education and growth, emphasising its role in fostering intellectual curiosity, adaptability, and personal fulfillment. Whether it is for career advancement, personal growth, or societal impact, investing in ongoing learning enables individuals to stay relevant, expand their horizons, and make meaningful contributions to both their personal lives and the world around them.

By actively pursuing new knowledge and experiences, individuals can not only maintain their competitive edge in a fast-paced global environment but also cultivate a sense of satisfaction and purpose. Adapting to a dynamic and unpredictable world requires a commitment to lifelong learning.

The importance of lifelong learning

Learning new things throughout one's life has several benefits that improve many aspects of one's life, including one's career and personal development. Here's why it is crucial:

Adaptability: As technology continues to reshape industries and job roles, the ability to adapt to change has become essential. Lifelong learning equips individuals with up-to-date knowledge and relevant skills, allowing them to navigate shifts in the job market and meet new challenges head-on. Whether it is learning new technology, understanding market trends, or developing leadership skills, lifelong learners remain flexible and resilient in an uncertain world.

Intellectual curiosity: Lifelong learning fosters a natural sense of curiosity, pushing individuals to explore new ideas and challenge long-held beliefs. It inspires intellectual exploration, encouraging individuals to ask questions, seek deeper understanding, and view the world through different lenses. This mindset of continuous inquiry not only leads to personal growth but also enhances critical thinking and problem-solving abilities.

Personal fulfillment: Engaging in ongoing learning provides a sense of accomplishment and purpose. Whether you are pursuing a hobby, learning a new language, or diving deeper into a field of interest, lifelong learning fuels personal passions and supports emotional well-being. It offers opportunities for self-discovery, helping individuals better understand their strengths, values, and aspirations.

Social impact: Lifelong learning doesn't just benefit the individual. It has a broader societal impact. Well-informed and educated individuals are better equipped to contribute to their communities, engage in civic discussions, and advocate for social change. By staying informed on global issues, participating in community activities, and contributing innovative ideas, lifelong learners play an important role in shaping the future of society.

Types of Continuing Education

Lifelong learning encompasses a broad range of learning experiences, each offering its own unique set of benefits. The various forms of continuing education cover the following areas:

Formal education: It includes structured academic programs such as degrees, certifications, and professional development courses. Whether pursuing higher education, attending workshops, or completing specialised training, formal education provides learners with recognised credentials and helps build a solid foundation for career growth. Often, the focus is on acquiring specific knowledge or skills that are directly relevant to a profession or industry.

Informal education: Unlike formal education, informal learning happens outside traditional educational institutions and is often self-directed. It encompasses online courses, podcasts, webinars, reading, and even attending conferences or community lectures. Informal education allows learners to explore topics at their own pace, on their terms, and often based on personal interests. With the rise of digital platforms and educational resources, anyone can access a wide range of subjects and develop skills at their convenience.

Experiential learning: This hands-on approach involves learning through direct experience, including internships, volunteer work, travel, and real-world problem-solving. Experiential learning imparts practical knowledge and skills that the classroom often fails to impart. It encourages learners to take risks, make mistakes, and develop a deeper understanding of subjects through personal involvement. It is an excellent way to translate theoretical knowledge into actionable insights, making it particularly valuable for career development.

Benefits of Continuing Education

Engaging in lifelong learning offers a wealth of benefits that impact various facets of an individual's life.

Career advancement: While retirees may not require this benefit, individuals in the age range of 40 to 50 years can greatly benefit from it. Factors such as delays in investing for various goals make this benefit especially relevant. Bridging the skill set gap, if any, through education can advance one's career, especially with limited time available before retirement and a multitude of tasks to complete. In today's fast-changing job market, continuous learning is a strategic tool for career progression. By staying current with industry trends, mastering new technologies, or acquiring specialised skills, lifelong learners position themselves for promotions, salary increases, or new job opportunities.

Enhanced employability: Lifelong learners stand out in a competitive job market. By demonstrating the initiative to learn new skills, whether through formal education or informal means, they present themselves as adaptable, innovative, and forward-thinking. After retirement, this benefit could be crucial for individuals seeking meaningful full-time or part-time employment, especially if they need to bridge skill gaps. Many employers look for maturity and experience; therefore, if there is a small skill gap, for example, in learning computer skills, then that can be bridged, and it will be an unbeatable combination.

Personal growth: Lifelong learning isn't just about career development - it is also a pathway to self-improvement. By pursuing knowledge, individuals gain a deeper understanding of themselves and the world around them. Exploring new subjects, from philosophy to coding, allows individuals to break out of their comfort zones, gain fresh perspectives, and expand their intellectual and emotional horizons. Age should never be a barrier to continuous education.

Increased confidence: As individuals acquire new skills and knowledge, they often experience a boost in self-confidence. This newfound confidence spills over into all areas of life, from personal relationships to social interactions. Confident learners are more willing to take on new challenges, engage in meaningful conversations, and embrace growth opportunities.

Strategies for successful lifelong learning

To maximise the benefits of lifelong learning, individuals need to adopt effective strategies that keep them motivated and engaged. Here are some key approaches:

Set clear goals: Establish specific learning objectives to keep yourself focused. Whether it is earning a new certification or mastering a new hobby, having a clear goal in mind helps you stay on track and measure your progress.

Find your learning style: Everyone has a preferred way of learning. Whether you are a visual learner who benefits from diagrams, an auditory learner who enjoys podcasts, or a kinesthetic learner who needs hands-on practice, understanding your learning style can help you choose the most effective study methods.

Utilise resources: Take advantage of the numerous resources available for lifelong learning. From free online courses offered by platforms like Coursera and Khan Academy to local workshops and public libraries, opportunities to learn something new are virtually endless. Many universities also offer non-credit courses or continuing education programs open to the public.

Create a supportive environment: Surround yourself with people who support and encourage your learning journey. This might involve joining study groups, attending seminars, or finding a mentor who can offer guidance and motivation. A strong support network can make the learning process more enjoyable and sustainable.

Prioritise self-care: We need to ensure that we take care of your mental and physical well-being throughout the learning process. Sufficient rest, proper nutrition, and regular exercise are key factors in maintaining cognitive function and overall productivity. A well-balanced lifestyle supports better learning outcomes.

The inspiring story of a lawyer

Mrs. Archana Bhardwaj (name changed) had always wanted to be a lawyer. She began studying law after completing her graduation at the age of 22. However, her parents' desire for an early marriage compelled her to withdraw from her LLB course just 6 months after her enrollment. After marriage, her passion for studying law remained, while she continued to be busy with her family and raising her two children. In 2020, it had been 25 years since she left the LLB course. Both her children were independent and did not need her day-to-day support. She returned to the course to pursue her LLB and has now followed her dream of becoming a lawyer at the age of 51. Education should never end; we should always learn something new. If we do not learn, then we stop growing.

———————∞———————

Key takeaways

- Lifelong learning is not just a trend. It is a crucial element of personal and professional development in today's world.
- By embracing a continuous learning mindset, individuals can remain adaptable, relevant, and fulfilled in an ever-changing environment.
- Whether through formal education, informal self-directed study, or hands-on experiences, lifelong learning empowers individuals to grow both personally and professionally.

- Growing yourself, your career, and your communities is a future investment.
- As the world continues to evolve, those who remain committed to learning will find themselves better equipped to navigate life's challenges and seize new opportunities.

8

Travel Adventures: Exploring New Horizons

Retirement means more time for adventure. Your adventure outside the 9-5 starts today.

In this chapter, we will embark on an exploration of the exhilarating world of travel adventures, where curiosity meets the unknown and discovery becomes a way of life. Adventure travel is about more than just visiting new places. It is about immersing yourself in diverse cultures, pushing personal boundaries, and embracing the thrill of new experiences. Adventure travel offers a dynamic mix of excitement, learning, and transformation, whether you are hiking through untamed landscapes, diving into deep seas, or immersing yourself in the rhythm of bustling cities. As we journey through this chapter, we will uncover the many layers of adventure, from the physical challenges that test your endurance to the mental and emotional growth that comes with exploring new cultures. You will learn how travel can shape perspectives, create lifelong memories, and open up new realms of possibility in your life.

The allure of adventure travel

Adventure travel has a unique allure, offering an extraordinary blend of physical activity, cultural immersion, and the deep satisfaction that comes from conquering the unknown. What makes adventure travel so special is the opportunity to step outside the mundane and familiar into environments that challenge your body, stimulate your mind, and enrich your soul.

For some, adventure travel is synonymous with adrenaline - whether it is scaling towering peaks, diving into the ocean's depths, or skydiving from the clouds. These intense physical experiences offer a rush like no other. For others, adventure is about connecting with nature in its most pristine and untouched form, whether it is through hiking or challenging activities. Hiking in mountains or paddling through remote rivers far from civilization's reach are examples of challenging activities. Adventure travel also offers something even more profound: the chance to experience cultures, traditions, and ways of life that are vastly different from your own. This immersion fosters greater understanding and compassion as you learn to see the world through new eyes.

In every sense, adventure travel encourages you to push your limits, whether physical, emotional, or mental. It challenges you to adapt, learn, and grow, offering a refreshing departure from the routines of daily life and creating memories that last long after the journey is over.

Popular adventure travel destinations

Adventure travel can take many forms, and the world is full of destinations that cater to every type of thrill-seeker. Whether you are drawn to towering mountain peaks, the tranquillity of tropical beaches, or the raw beauty of wilderness areas, there is an adventure waiting for you. Some of the most popular adventure travel destinations are as follows:

Mountains and hiking: For those drawn to the majesty of the mountains, places like the Himalayas, Alps, and Andes offer not only breathtaking scenery but also a range of hikes that cater to both the casual trekker and the seasoned mountaineer. Whether you seek the challenge of summiting Everest or prefer a less extreme but equally scenic trek through the Swiss Alps, the mountains provide an unparalleled adventure experience.

Beaches and islands: The world's most beautiful beaches and islands, from the Caribbean to the Maldives and Southeast Asia, are ideal destinations for those looking to combine adventure with relaxation. Adventure activities in these areas include snorkelling among coral reefs, diving to explore shipwrecks, surfing world-class waves, or simply enjoying the beauty of the natural world with a day of paddle boarding or beach hiking.

Wilderness and wildlife: If encountering exotic wildlife in its natural habitat excites you, there are few better options than exploring regions like the Amazon rainforest, the African savanna, or the Australian Outback. Here, you can witness animals in their natural environments. Experience the thrill of tracking lions in the Serengeti, spotting jaguars in the Amazon, or witnessing kangaroos bounding across the red sands of the Outback.

Cultural experiences: Adventure travel doesn't always have to be about nature and extreme activities. Many adventurers seek the thrill of cultural discovery by immersing themselves in different cultures. themselves in different cultures. themselves in ancient civilizations, traditional villages, and bustling cities. Exploring Machu Picchu, wandering through the temples of Angkor Wat, or navigating the lively streets of Marrakech can offer equally enriching and exciting experiences, feeding both your curiosity and your soul.

Extreme sports: For adrenaline junkies, adventure travel can take the form of high-octane activities such as bungee jumping over Victoria Falls, skydiving in New Zealand, whitewater rafting through the Grand Canyon, or paragliding off cliffs in Brazil. These experiences aim to challenge your body and mind, providing thrills that few other experiences can equal.

Planning your adventure

Before embarking on an adventure, careful planning is essential to ensure a smooth and rewarding experience.

Unlike typical vacations, adventure travel often requires more preparation, from understanding the physical demands to ensuring your safety. Here are some key steps to consider when planning your next adventure:

Choose your destination: Start by considering what type of adventure appeals to you the most. Do you want to challenge yourself physically with a strenuous trek, or would you prefer to engage with new cultures? Once you have narrowed down your interests, consider your budget and available time, which will help you finalise your destination.

Research activities: After choosing your destination, delve deeper into the specific activities available. For example, if you are heading to the Himalayas for a trek, you will want to know the best routes, what permits are required, and the level of difficulty. For water-based adventures, it is important to research the weather and conditions at different times of the year.

Plan your itinerary: Having a clear and well-structured itinerary is crucial, especially for adventure travel. Your itinerary should include not only your activities but also time for rest, travel between locations, and any contingency plans for unforeseen events, such as adverse weather.

Pack appropriately: Adventure travel often involves lightweight packing, as many activities require mobility and carrying your gear. Make sure to pack only the essentials, including the right clothing, gear for your specific activities, and any health and safety items you might need.

Consider safety: Always prioritise your safety by researching your destination's safety conditions. This entails comprehending the political stability of your destination, as well as any potential health risks. required vaccinations, and the risk of natural hazards. It is also essential to have appropriate travel insurance that covers adventure activities.

The benefits of adventure travel

The benefits of adventure travel go far beyond the momentary thrill. It offers long-lasting physical, mental, and emotional rewards that can enrich your life in profound ways. Here are some of the most significant benefits:

Physical fitness: Adventure sports like mountain climbing, kayaking, and hiking are excellent ways to strengthen your body. The physical obstacles give you a thrilling sense of accomplishment and help you gain strength, endurance, and general fitness.

Stress reduction: Physical activity and time spent in nature are tried-and-true ways to lower stress and anxiety. Adventure travel offers an organic getaway from the stresses of daily life, enabling you to refuel and achieve mental clarity.

Personal growth: Stepping out of your comfort zone and facing new challenges builds resilience and fosters personal growth. Each adventure allows you to discover more about yourself, overcome fears, and gain a deeper sense of confidence and independence.

Cultural immersion: By travelling to new and unfamiliar places, you gain firsthand experience of different cultures, traditions, and ways of life. This exposure not only broadens your perspective but also helps foster empathy, respect, and a greater appreciation for the diversity of the world.

Lifelong memories: The stories and experiences you gain from adventure travel often become some of your most treasured memories. Whether it is standing at the top of a mountain after a long trek or sharing a meal with locals in a remote village, these moments stay with you, shaping your worldview and enriching your life.

Still not convinced about adventure travel?

This story, published in HuffPost on September 7, 2024, will undoubtedly inspire you. Mr. Ashok Shenolikar, an 84-year-old veteran, and his wife Bharati take adventure travel regularly in their retirement. He is a retired engineer, novelist, short story writer, and essayist based in Ellicott City, Maryland, USA. He shares his insights on living a healthy, fulfilling life. He credits his longevity to staying active, both physically and mentally, maintaining strong relationships, and continuously travelling the world. His tips include not procrastinating on goals, adjusting to physical changes with age, and keeping a busy mind through hobbies like writing and learning languages. He emphasises the importance of maintaining friendships and avoiding unnecessary conflict while cherishing moments with loved ones. Overall, Shenolikar's approach is about living with purpose, adaptability, and connection. To read the complete story, please check out this link: https://bit.ly/Ashok-Shenolikar. I hope this inspires all those who are already retired and want to travel.

Key takeaways

- Adventure travel offers a rich and rewarding experience that transcends the ordinary.
- Whether you are in search of physical challenges, cultural discovery, or a chance to connect with nature, adventure travel provides an opportunity to step outside your daily routine and immerse yourself in the unknown.
- By embracing the spirit of exploration, planning carefully, and being open to new experiences, you can embark on a journey that not only enriches your life but also leaves you with unforgettable memories.
- Adventure is out there, waiting. Are you ready to take the first step?

9

Finding Purpose: Discovering Your Life's Mission

"Retirement is not a life without purpose; it is the ongoing purpose that provides meaningfulness" – Robert Rivers

In the rich tapestry of life, each thread tells a story woven from experiences, passions, and aspirations. Yet, many of us, at some point, feel a sense of being adrift, as though the deeper meaning of our existence is elusive. The search for purpose is one of the most profound and transformative journeys a person can undertake. It is not simply about achieving success or ticking off life's milestones but about finding a driving force that infuses your life with meaning, direction, and fulfillment. This chapter delves into this crucial quest for personal purpose, offering insights into how you can discover your life's mission, align it with your daily actions, and cultivate a sense of deep satisfaction and resilience, even when challenges arise.

Understanding purpose

The purpose is much more than a fleeting goal or a

momentary ambition. It is a compass that directs you through life's twists and turns. At its core, purpose is the integration of your deepest values, passions, and contributions to the world. It gives meaning to your efforts and provides a sense of fulfillment beyond material success. Purpose often manifests as a desire to make a positive impact on others or the world, aligning your inner beliefs with external actions.

While purpose can shift and evolve as you grow and learn, having a foundational sense of direction is essential. Without purpose, life can feel like a series of disjointed actions, but with it, even the simplest moments gain a sense of significance. The beauty of purpose is that it doesn't have to be grand or earth-shattering. It can be as simple as living with kindness, fostering community, or nurturing creativity. The key is that it fits your values and identity.

Self-Reflection and Discovery

Discovering your purpose requires thoughtful reflection and a willingness to explore your inner world. This process takes time, patience, and self-awareness, but it can illuminate the path toward a more meaningful life. Here are several strategies to guide you on this journey of self-discovery:

Values assessment: Your values serve as the foundation of your purpose. Reflect on the principles that guide your decisions and behaviours. Ask yourself: What do you stand for? What principles do you want to uphold in both your personal and professional life? Are there particular causes or issues you feel strongly about, such as social justice, environmental sustainability, or compassion for others?

Passion exploration: Discovering what excites you is key to finding purpose. Take note of the activities that naturally energise you. What topics make you lose track of time? Is there something you can do for hours without feeling exhausted or bored? Passions often point toward a deeper purpose as they reveal where your heart and mind feel most alive.

Skills inventory: Your unique talents and skills are clues to your purpose. These are the abilities you have honed over time, both through deliberate practice and natural aptitude. Are you a gifted communicator, problem solver, or artist? Consider how you can use your strengths to improve your own or others' lives.

Life experiences: Pivotal moments often shape our worldview and influence our sense of purpose. Reflect on past experiences that have had a lasting impact on you. Have some specific challenges or victories helped you grow? Sometimes, the difficulties we face are the very things that lead us toward our purpose, as they give us insight into what truly matters.

Visualisation is a powerful exercise in finding purpose. Imagine your ideal future. Visualise yourself living a life of fulfillment. What does that look like? Are you working in a field that excites you, making a meaningful contribution to your community, or leading a life rich in personal connections? This vision can act as a guidepost, helping you to steer toward the life you aspire to live.

Finding meaningful work

For many, purpose and career intersect, and finding meaningful work can be a critical part of living a purposeful life. However, this doesn't imply that you must entirely shift your career path or undertake a major endeavour. Meaningful work is about aligning your professional life with your values, passions, and skills. Here are some strategies for doing just that:

Align values and passions: Seek career opportunities that resonate with your values and ignite your passions. This doesn't necessarily mean you have to work for a nonprofit or a cause-based organisation; many roles can offer purpose if they allow you to live according to your core values and contribute in a way that feels meaningful.

Explore different paths: If your current job doesn't align with your sense of purpose, consider exploring new career paths. This doesn't require a dramatic change - volunteering, freelancing, or taking on side projects can provide new insights and allow you to experiment with different roles. These experiences can serve as stepping stones toward a more fulfilling career.

Continuous learning: Purpose often requires growth and adaptation. By continuing to learn and develop professionally, you not only enhance your skills but also stay open to new opportunities that align with your purpose. Lifelong learning can also introduce you to new passions and help you refine your sense of mission.

Overcoming Challenges

The road to finding your purpose is not always straightforward. It is a journey filled with self-doubt, moments of uncertainty, and periods of confusion. However, these challenges are a natural part of the process and offer important lessons along the way. Here are some ways to navigate these challenges:

Embrace uncertainty: It is normal to feel unsure about your purpose, especially at the beginning. Rather than rushing to find all the answers, allow yourself to live in the uncertainty for a while. Purpose evolves with time, and it's okay if you don't have it all figured out immediately.

Seek support: Surround yourself with supportive individuals who can offer guidance and encouragement. Whether it is a mentor, coach, or close friend, having someone to share your journey with can provide clarity and motivation.

Practice gratitude: Cultivating appreciation is an effective way to shift your focus from what's lacking to what's already abundant in your life. Acknowledging the positive aspects of your life, no matter how small, can help you maintain an optimistic mindset during challenging times.

Be patient: Discovering your purpose is not a one-time event but an ongoing process. Be patient with yourself as you explore different paths and experiences. Even small progress is worth celebrating, and trust that your purpose will emerge over time.

A very inspiring story of having a purpose

A tribe in the mountains kidnaps a baby. Despite their best efforts, the lowland tribe's strongest men fail to climb the mountain to rescue the child. However, the baby's mother successfully retrieves her child and descends the mountain. When asked how she managed it, she simply responds, "It wasn't your baby." The story highlights the power of a mother's determination and love, which can surpass even the greatest physical challenges.

(Source: www.purposefocuscommitment.com).

—∞—

Key takeaways

- The journey to discovering your purpose is one of the most rewarding paths you can embark upon.
- It requires introspection, patience, and a willingness to explore your passions, values, and talents.
- Purpose is not a fixed destination; it is a continuous process of growth and self-discovery.
- As you engage in this exploration, you will not only cultivate a deeper sense of meaning but also contribute to the world in a way that is uniquely yours.
- Embrace the uncertainty, trust the process, and let your life's mission unfold one step at a time.

10
Embracing Serenity: Cultivating Inner Peace

"If you look at what you have in life, you'll always have more. If you look at what you don't have in life, you'll never have enough." - Oprah Winfrey

In today's fast-paced and constantly evolving world, moments of peace and calm can feel like fleeting luxuries. The rapid pace of modern life, with its endless demands, distractions, and pressures, often leaves little room for stillness and reflection. Yet, the pursuit of inner peace and serenity is not merely a desire for a break from the chaos. It is an essential component of our well-being. Inner peace enables us to navigate the ups and downs of life with greater ease, resilience, and joy. This chapter will explore practical, effective strategies for cultivating a sense of calm and balance, helping you to find tranquillity during life's inevitable storms.

Understanding serenity

Serenity is not simply the absence of stress, nor is it a passive state of detachment. True serenity is an active, intentional state of mind - a deep, abiding sense of peace and harmony within yourself, regardless of external circumstances. It is a state where you feel centered and grounded, allowing you to face challenges with clarity and grace. Serenity gives you the mental and emotional space to reflect, make better decisions, and foster meaningful connections with others. When we cultivate serenity, we not only enhance our sense of well-being but also improve our physical health, emotional stability, and relationships. It provides a foundation for greater contentment and joy in everyday life.

Mindfulness and Meditation

One of the main components of developing peace is mindfulness, which is the practice of being present and involved in the moment. It entails observing your thoughts, emotions, and environment objectively. By breaking the cycle of tension, worry, and overthinking, mindfulness practice enables you to stay grounded even during chaos.

Meditation allows one to cultivate mindfulness in the most efficient way possible. There are many different types of meditation, such as the ones listed below:

To focus your mind and calm your body, guided meditation requires listening to a sequence of instructions or visualisations.

Guided meditation involves following a guided visualisation or series of instructions to focus your mind and relax your body.

Mindfulness meditation: Focusses on staying present by concentrating on your breath, bodily sensations, or environment.

Loving-kindness meditation: Involves sending positive thoughts and compassion toward yourself and others. Regular meditation practice can rewire the brain to enhance focus, reduce anxiety, and increase overall feelings of calm. Even just a few minutes of meditation each day can create noticeable improvements in your mental clarity and emotional resilience.

Nature connection

There is a unique, soothing power in nature that can help us recalibrate and reconnect with our inner calm. Studies have shown that spending time in natural surroundings, whether in a forest, by the ocean, or in a simple park, lowers cortisol levels, the hormone associated with stress. Nature encourages mindfulness; whether you are listening to the rustle of leaves, watching a sunset, or feeling the warmth of the sun on your skin, these moments help you escape from the hustle of daily life and return to the simplicity and beauty of the present moment.

Even small interactions with nature, such as keeping a

plant in your home, going for a short walk, or sitting by a window to observe the clouds, can help cultivate serenity. Nature not only provides tranquillity but also helps remind us of our place within a larger, more interconnected world, encouraging a sense of peace and perspective.

Healthy lifestyle habits

Physical health and mental serenity are deeply intertwined. When our bodies are healthy and well-nourished, our minds are better equipped to handle stress and emotional challenges. Cultivating serenity requires not just mental and emotional practices but also a healthy lifestyle that supports overall well-being.

Exercise: Regular physical activity is one of the most effective ways to boost your mood and relieve stress. Whether it is walking, yoga, swimming, or weight training, exercise releases endorphins - chemicals that naturally improve your sense of well-being and reduce anxiety.

Sleep: Quality sleep is essential for mental and emotional stability. It is during sleep that your body restores itself and your mind processes the emotions and experiences of the day. A well-rested mind is more resilient, focussed, and capable of handling challenges with grace.

Nutrition: What you eat has a profound impact on how

you feel. A balanced diet rich in fruits, vegetables, whole grains, and healthy fats supports brain function and can stabilise mood and energy levels, promoting a more serene state of mind.

Hydration: Drinking enough water helps keep your body functioning properly, supporting both physical and cognitive processes that help maintain emotional balance.

Mindset shifts

Your mindset: -The way you think about yourself and the world plays a major role in your sense of serenity. By consciously adopting a positive and resilient mindset, you can better manage stress and foster inner peace, regardless of external circumstances.

Gratitude: Practicing gratitude shifts your focus from what's lacking in your life to what you already have. By regularly acknowledging and appreciating the small joys in life, you cultivate a sense of abundance and contentment, reducing the grip of stress and dissatisfaction.

Forgiveness: Holding onto grudges or past hurts creates emotional tension and disrupts your peace of mind. Practicing forgiveness, both toward others and yourself, can release these negative emotions, allowing you to move forward with greater freedom and calm.

Self-compassion: Treating yourself with kindness and understanding, especially during difficult times, can help you cultivate inner peace. Instead of being overly critical, embrace self-compassion as a way to soften your inner dialogue and support your emotional well-being.

Stress management techniques

While stress is unavoidable, it doesn't have to rule your life. Through the acquisition of good stress management strategies, you can mitigate the effects on your physical and mental health. Some proven techniques include:

Deep breathing exercises: Slow, deep breathing activates the body's relaxation response, calming the nervous system and reducing the physiological effects of stress.

Progressive muscle relaxation: This technique involves systematically tensing and relaxing different muscle groups in your body to release tension and promote relaxation.

Journalling: Writing about your thoughts and feelings can provide clarity and emotional release, helping you to process stress and gain perspective.

Building healthy relationships

Healthy relationships are a cornerstone of emotional well-being and serenity. When we feel supported and connected, we are better able to manage stress and maintain a sense of peace. Strong relationships provide comfort, validation, and a sense of belonging, all of which contribute to a more serene life. To foster healthy relationships:

Nurture connection: Spend time with loved ones who uplift and support you. Regular communication and shared experiences strengthen bonds and contribute to emotional well-being.

Set boundaries: Clear boundaries are necessary for healthy relationships. By setting limits on toxic behaviour and protecting your emotional space, you can maintain a sense of calm and safety in your interactions with others.

Finding meaning and purpose

A life filled with meaning and purpose naturally fosters inner peace. When your actions align with your core values and your life has direction, you are less likely to feel overwhelmed by day-to-day stresses. Meaning and purpose can come from various sources, such as personal relationships, work, creative pursuits, or contributing to a cause you care about.

Explore your values: Reflect on what matters most to you and how you can incorporate those values into your daily life. Aligning your actions with your values will bring a greater sense of fulfillment and peace, whether through your career, hobbies, or personal relationships.

Give back: Helping others can be a profound source of inner peace. Whether through volunteering, mentoring, or simply offering support to those around you, contributing to the well-being of others fosters a sense of connection and purpose.

Serenity by James Allen: A Beautiful Story

Calmness of mind is a powerful reflection of wisdom, achieved through self-control and understanding of oneself and others. This tranquillity stems from recognising the connection between thoughts and actions, allowing one to remain composed in the face of life's challenges. A calm person exudes strength, gaining trust and admiration from others. Serenity, the pinnacle of character development, is more valuable than wealth and brings lasting peace. In contrast, a lack of self-control leads to chaos and unhappiness, while mastering one's thoughts brings true power and harmony. (Credit: James Allen, Author)

Key takeaways

- Cultivating serenity is a lifelong journey that requires consistent practice, patience, and self-awareness.
- By incorporating mindfulness, nature, healthy habits, positive mindset shifts, and meaningful relationships into your daily life, you can create a foundation of inner peace that will carry you through life's inevitable challenges.
- Serenity is not a fixed destination but a state of being that you can nurture and grow. Each person's path to serenity is unique, so experiment with different techniques and approaches to discover what works best for you.
- With time and dedication, you can cultivate a deep, abiding sense of peace, no matter what life brings your way.

Conclusion

Second Innings on Your Terms provided a profound and insightful roadmap for individuals navigating the often uncertain yet promising phase of life that begins after the conclusion of their professional careers. We discussed in-depth of complexities and transitions that accompany retirement, presenting you with a holistic guide to managing the challenges and seizing the opportunities that come with this significant life change. More than just a handbook on retirement planning, I hope this book explores how individuals can redefine their identity, rekindle passions, and find deeper purpose once they step away from their careers.

The central theme of the book is transformation. Retirement is not simply the end of one's professional life but rather the beginning of a new, uncharted chapter - one that has the potential to be just as enriching and fulfilling, if not more so. By focussing on personal growth, meaningful pursuits, and lifestyle choices that align with individual values, I trust the book provided a positive framework for embracing this stage of life. Viewing retirement as an opportunity to reinvent, explore new interests, and engage with the world differently is a more appropriate perspective.

The book highlighted an important aspect of this transition: the emotional and psychological adjustment required during retirement. For many, the transition from a structured work routine to unstructured time can be overwhelming due to the deep intertwining of professional and personal identities. The absence of work can leave retirees grappling with feelings of purposelessness, loss, or confusion. **Second Innings on Your Terms** addresses these issues head-on, offering readers reassurance and guidance on how to navigate the emotional rollercoaster that sometimes accompanies the retirement experience.

The book emphasises the importance of staying mentally and physically active in retirement. It offered practical strategies for maintaining a vibrant and engaged lifestyle, whether that means pursuing hobbies, volunteering, learning new skills, or even embarking on a second career. Retirement is not a one-size-fits-all experience; each individual's journey is unique. As such, I encourage everyone to reflect on their desires, interests, and personal definitions of success rather than adhering to societal expectations or norms.

In addition to providing insight into the personal aspects of retirement, I also delved into the social dynamics that often change during this period. Relationships with family, friends, and community members can evolve, and we need to nurture these connections. Retirement can be an ideal time to strengthen bonds with loved ones or even build new relationships through shared interests or community involvement. It can also be a time to focus on self-care and personal well-being, as retirees have the freedom to prioritise their own needs after years of focusing on work and other responsibilities.

While financial stability is undoubtedly a critical component of a successful retirement, money alone does not equate to happiness or fulfillment. We emphasise the importance of developing a comprehensive retirement plan that encompasses financial, emotional, physical, and social aspects. We encourage you to approach retirement with a balanced mindset, ensuring that they have not only the financial resources to support themselves but also the emotional and social support systems needed to thrive.

I believe what sets this book apart from other retirement books is its emphasis on the broader concept of purpose. It goes beyond the surface-level advice often found in retirement planning books and instead digs into the deeper question of how individuals can lead lives of purpose and significance after they retire. Whether through mentoring, community involvement, artistic endeavours, or spiritual growth, the book offers a variety of pathways for readers to explore as they seek to infuse their retirement years with meaning.

I hope the inclusion of real-life stories and anecdotes throughout the book served as a source of inspiration. These stories illustrated how others have successfully navigated the transition into retirement, providing relatable examples of the triumphs and challenges that come with this life change. The diversity of experiences showcased in the book reflects the myriad ways that individuals can approach retirement, reinforcing the idea that there is no right or wrong way to retire - only the way that feels most authentic and fulfilling to the individual.

The book is a guide to living life on one's own terms. I hope it empowers you to take charge of your post-career journey, offering the tools, insights, and encouragement needed to make the most of this phase. Retirement is portrayed not as an end but as a beginning - an opportunity to create a life that is rich in experiences, relationships, and personal satisfaction. By embracing this mindset, we can move forward with confidence, knowing that their best years may still lie ahead.

Life is a continuous process of growth and change, and retirement is simply another stage in that journey. With the right mindset and approach, this stage can be one of the most rewarding and fulfilling of all. I hope that with my practical advice, you will be equipped to face the challenges of retirement head-on while remaining open to the incredible possibilities that await in this exciting new chapter of life. I envision this book serving as a guide for achieving both personal and financial prosperity. I hope that after reading this book, you will embrace your second innings with optimism, curiosity, and a renewed sense of purpose. If this occurs, I believe I have achieved the goal of writing this book.

Navigating the transition from work to play!

Rajesh Minocha, an MBA (Finance) and CFP®, has 21+ years of experience with ICICI & Franklin Templeton. Gaining financial freedom at 45, he founded Financial Radiance in 2016 and now manages 350+ portfolios while conducting global investor education programs.

Schedule a meeting with me today!
Scan the QR code to get started.

Ready to take on your future?
Visit: www.financialradiance.com
www.rajeshminocha.com